Contents

I am a firefighter

My name is Dwight.
I am a firefighter.

I work for the
Hertfordshire Fire
and Rescue Service.

PEOPLE WHO HELP US

FIREFIGHTER

Rebecca Hunter

**Photography by
Chris Fairclough**

CHERRYTREE BOOKS

A Cherrytree book

First published in paperback in 2011 by
Evans Brothers Ltd
2A Portman Mansions
Chiltern Street
London W1U 6NR

British Library Cataloguing in Publication Data
Hunter, Rebecca
   Fire Fighter. - (People who help us)
   1. Physicians - Juvenile literature
   I. Title
   363. 3'78

ISBN 9781842346259

Planned and produced by Discovery Books Ltd
Editor: Rebecca Hunter
Designer: Ian Winton
© Evans Brothers Ltd 2005

Acknowledgements
Photographs on p 5 and p 19 (top) reproduced with kind permission of Dave Humphreys of the Hertfordshire Fire & Rescue Service.
All other photography by Chris Fairclough.

The author, packager and publisher would like to thank Dwight Williams and all other members of the Hertfordshire Fire & Rescue Service for their participation in this book.

Printed in India by Nutech Print Services.

Words appearing in bold **like this**, are explained in the glossary.

Firefighters put out fires, but we also provide many other useful **services**. This book shows you some of the things we do.

The morning parade

Firefighters need to be able to answer emergency call-outs, twenty-four hours a day. This means we have two shifts of duty; the day shift and the night shift.

Today I am on the day shift. I start work at nine o'clock.

HEMEL HEMPSTEAD
FIRE STATION

◆

HERTFORDSHIRE
FIRE & RESCUE
SERVICE

WORKING TO PROTECT
ACTING TO SAVE

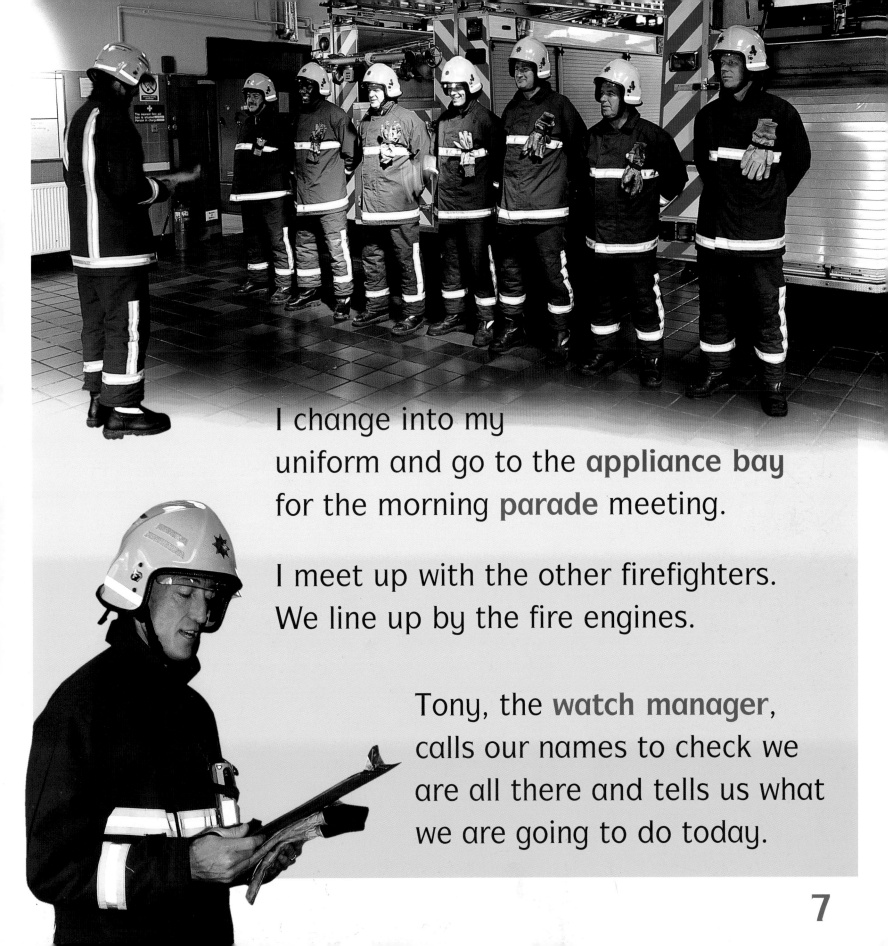

I change into my
uniform and go to the **appliance bay**
for the morning **parade** meeting.

I meet up with the other firefighters.
We line up by the fire engines.

Tony, the **watch manager**,
calls our names to check we
are all there and tells us what
we are going to do today.

Checking the equipment

Our first job of the day is to look over the fire engine and check all the **equipment**.

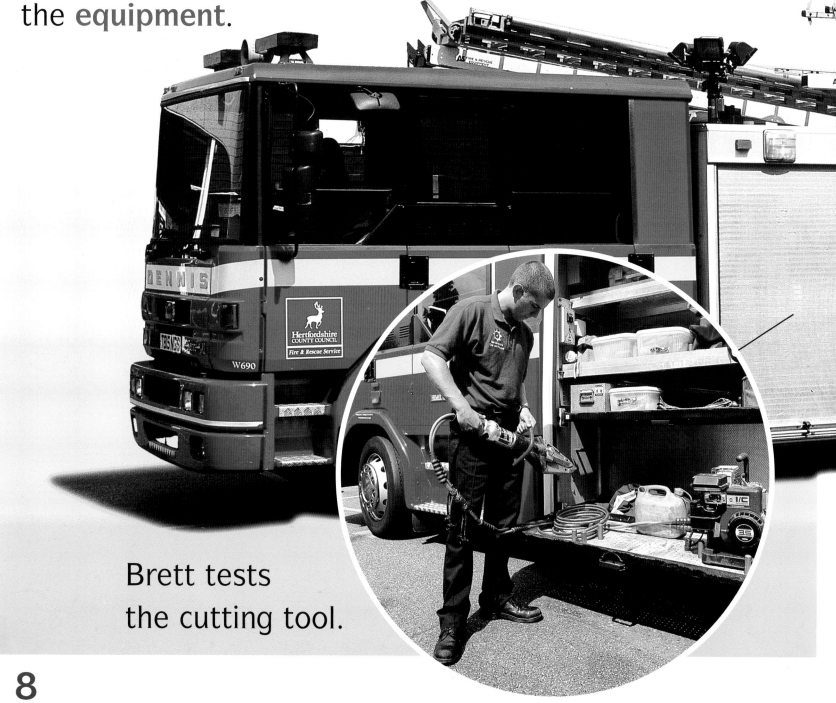

Brett tests the cutting tool.

I look at the list of equipment and check that everything is there.

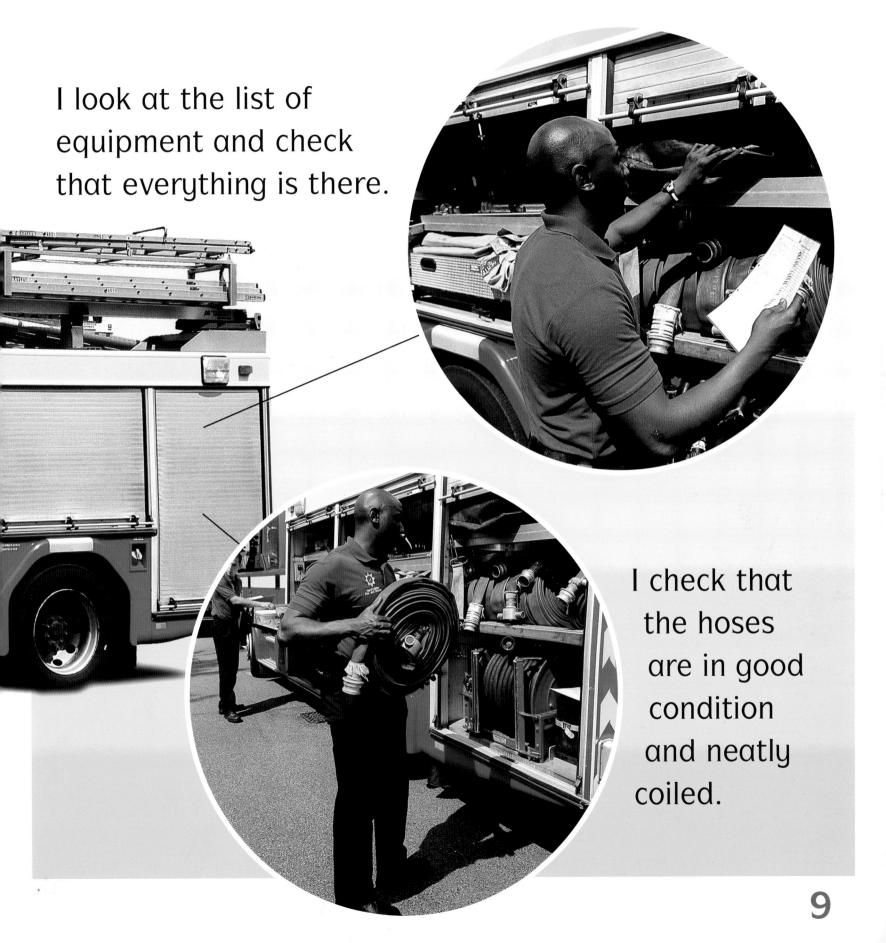

I check that the hoses are in good condition and neatly coiled.

Practical training

Now we are going to do some **practical training**. We must know how to use our equipment so that in an emergency we are ready for anything.

The ladders are very heavy. They are also very long. You need to have a good head for heights!

Next we practise going into a building that is on fire. We use breathing **apparatus** so the smoke will not affect us. Brett opens the door carefully. I am ready with the hose. The third officer keeps a note of how long we stay in the building.

School visit

Firefighters often visit schools to tell children about the fire service and how to prevent fires.

I talk to the class about smoke alarms. The fire service wants to make sure that every house has a smoke alarm.

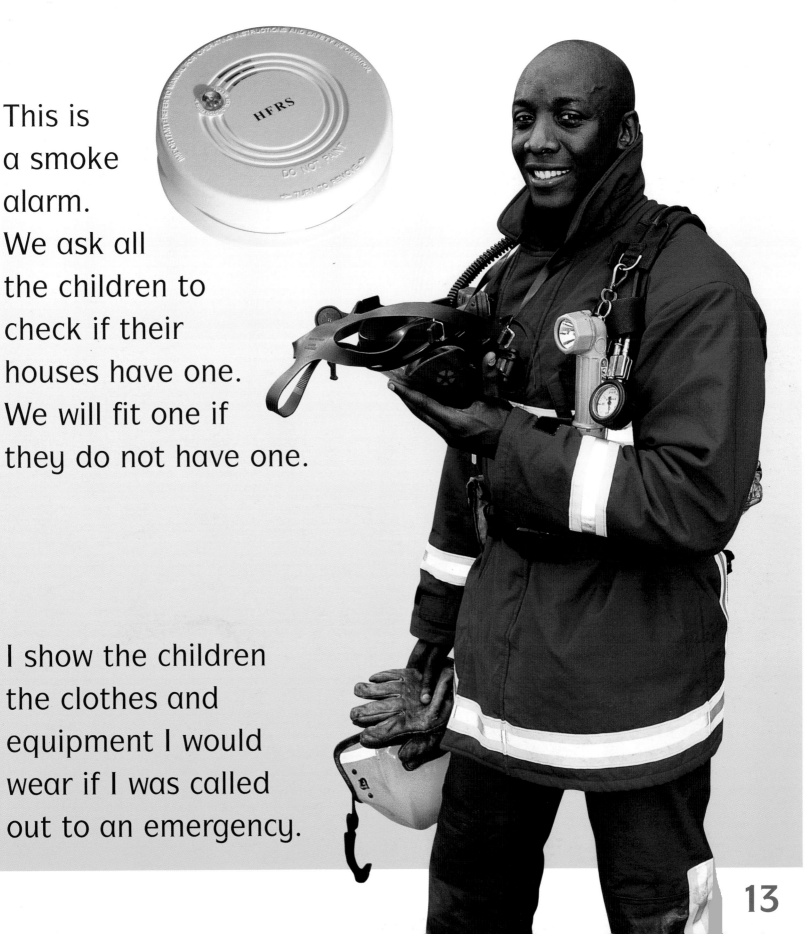

This is a smoke alarm. We ask all the children to check if their houses have one. We will fit one if they do not have one.

I show the children the clothes and equipment I would wear if I was called out to an emergency.

Fitting an alarm

Carol has a new baby. She is worried because she doesn't have a smoke alarm in her house. We are going to fit one for her.

We have to take the fire engine and full fire **crew** in case we are suddenly called out to an emergency.

We fit the smoke alarm on the ceiling at the top of the stairs. We tell Carol to test the battery every few months.

Carol signs a form to say we have done the work. She is much happier now.

Exercise and lunch

Before lunch I have some free time so I go down to our **gym**. It is important for a firefighter to be fit, so I like to exercise in the gym whenever I can.

At one o'clock we go to the **mess deck** for lunch.

I am on lunch duty today. It is my turn to help in the kitchen. After lunch I make everyone a cup of tea.

Road traffic accidents

Firefighters are often called out to accidents on the road. We call these road traffic accidents or RTAs. We may have to cut people out of their wrecked cars and sometimes give them **medical help**.

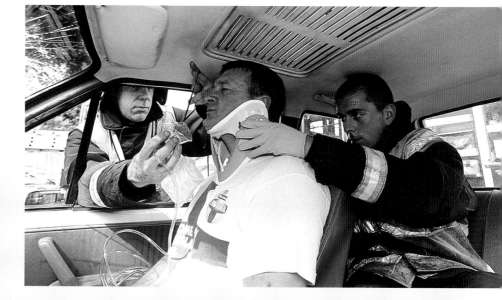

It is important to practise how to do this so we have set up a pretend accident scene.

I am learning how to cut the door frame off a car with the cutting tool.

This is a real road traffic accident.

Accidents like this need all three emergency services: fire, police and ambulance.

Call-out!

The alarm bell is going. It is an emergency!
We all run to the fire engine and put on our kit.

The duty man tears the turnout
sheet from the machine. This
tells us what sort of **incident**
it is and where we are going.

A tractor is on fire.
The engine is very hot
and might explode.
I spray it with water to
cool it down.

There is lots of **diesel** on
the road. We have
to call out the
Environment Agency.
They will come to
deal with the
spilled diesel
and stop it
polluting rivers
and streams.

Cleaning up

It is nearly six o'clock and time for me to go home. Before I go I help hose down the fire engines. Today has been a busy day.

My job is sometimes dangerous but often exciting. I do enjoy being a firefighter.

Glossary

apparatus the equipment used for a particular task

appliance bay the area where the fire engines are kept

crew people with special skills who work together to run something

diesel a type of fuel

emergency a serious situation that must be dealt with immediately

Environment Agency
an organization that helps look after our surroundings

equipment all the things that are needed for a particular job or activity

gym a room for sports and exercise. It is short for gymnasium.

incident an unusual event

medical help giving treatment to people who are ill or hurt

mess deck the dining room – from an old expression used on ships

parade a line of people waiting to be inspected or instructed

pollute to make something dirty

practical training learning how to do something by actually doing it

service when someone or an organization provides help

shift a set period during which people work

watch manager the person in charge of the shifts

Index